Lines of Flight

Lines of Flight

POEMS BY
Catherine Chandler

ABLE MUSE PRESS

Able Muse Press

www.ablemusepress.com

ISBN 978-0-9865338-3-9

Foreword copyright ©2011 by Rhina P. Espaillat

Cover image: *Dreamside* by silent-view.com

Cover & book design by Alexander Pepple

Able Muse Press is an imprint of *Able Muse*: A Review of Poetry, Prose & Art—at
www.ablemuse.com

Able Muse Press
467 Saratoga Avenue #602
San Jose, CA 95129
USA

for Hugo

Acknowledgments

The author gratefully acknowledges the publications in which these poems (sometimes with different titles) first appeared:

Able Muse: "Wing-stroke," "Drought," "99 Bottles of Beer on the Wall," "Supernova," "Delineations," "Flammarion Woodcut Pilgrim Redux." *Alabama Literary Review:* "The Loiterers (Of Diminished Things)." *The Barefoot Muse:* "66," "Joy Ride." *Blue Unicorn:* "Fatuity," "Assembly." *Candelabrum:* "Henslow's Sparrow," "Caesura." *The Cento: A Collection of Collage Poems* (Red Hen Press, 2011): "I Had Some Things." *The Centrifugal Eye:* "Lost and Found." *The Chimaera:* "Writ." *Comstock Review:* "Shadow Fish." *Dash Literary Journal:* "Gia Dinh." *First Things:* "Mother's Day" (reprinted in the anthology, *Grace Notes*), "Eleven." *The Flea:* "Hunger," "To the Lightning Bug," "∞." *14 by 14:* "Harrowing," "Setback," "In Nora's Garden (A Widow's Weeds)," "Where All the Ladders Start," "Marah's Waters (On the Beach at Piriápolis)," "Her Massive Sandal." *Fox Chase Review:* "Ballad of the Vernal Equinox," "Boots." *FutureCycle Poetry:* "Irène: A Portrait." *Hawk and Whippoorwill:* "Dandelion." *The HyperTexts:*

"New Hampshire Interval." *Measure:* "Missing," "Singularities." *Mezzo Cammin:* "Vermont Passage," "*sub rosa.*" *Möbius:* "Elderberry Tale (Elderberry)," "Endgame." *Orbis:* "Oneironaut." *Passages: A Collection of Poems by the Greenwood Poets:* "Prayer on the Pampas." *Poets Against War:* "Ruins (Aeons)." *The Raintown Review:* "The Deep Season," "The Gambler (A Gambler's Triolet)," "Spirit." *Shit Creek Review:* "To the Man on Mansfield Street." *Sonnetto Poesia:* "Matryoshka." *Soundzine:* "For My Granddaughter (For Moriah)," "Cinquefoil," "Docga." *Texas Poetry Journal:* "Susquehanna (Wilkes-Barre)." *Twigs and Leaves:* "Roses and Biscuits." *Umbrella Journal:* "Lines," "Ushuaia (The Dogs of Ushuaia)," "Madeleine Moment (Sapodilla)," "When in Lourdes."

The author also wishes to thank members of the *Eratosphere* online poetry workshop and members of the Greenwood Poets for their invaluable advice, encouragement and friendship; and her parents, Bernard and Bernice Chandler, for the gift of life and the gift of music.

Foreword

One of the things that poetry—when it's very good—does better than anything else is to suggest conflicting things at the same time and confront the reader with the possibility that both may be true. This book, which is extraordinarily good, does that to perfection.

Poem after poem, in dark, intelligent observations of human experience, demonstrates the "inexorable slaughter" that underlies life, while simultaneously noting that the slaughter is also "rational," and that, as in a poem titled "Lost and Found," some things do balance out, if only haphazardly:

> A key, a button, a leather glove.
> First love.
>
> A friend to cancer, a voice to grief.
> An old belief.
>
> An arrowhead, a perfect shell.
> The first bluebell.
>
> The river's source, a taste for ink.
> Hope, I think.

Catherine Chandler achieves the double vision conveyed by this list not by being duplicitous, but by acknowledging—and trying hard to accept—the duplicitousness of experience itself, the inevitable damage that reality works on our lives, and our hopeless and hopeful attachment to the world in which that damage takes place.

And what a great deal of damage these poems record: personal losses, political, inevitable and accidental "disappearances," the scars left by history under the green fields of home, the carnage to which the Vietnam Memorial, among so many, bears witness. Even our dreams, the poet suggests, flash us warnings as to the untrustworthiness of apparent safety. Even our joys—the pleasures of rearing children, for instance—are laced with risks, risks made real in such poems as "Cinquefoil," in which delicate flower imagery is blended with family history to describe how a daughter, after "her lilac love had passed away,"

> came home, crossed out her summer wedding day,
> chopped off her hair. Faded to grey.
>
> How can a mother's store of moss and cress
> soften the hell
> of marigold and asphodel?

There are comforts too, of course, if only the temporary joy of a family gathering, the unquestioning love of an old dog, or the speaker—the poet in the role of shopper, in "Fatuity"—refusing to apologize for the unwise purchases she knowingly makes at the supermarket of her daily life. In fact, Catherine Chandler implies that the most reliable and sustaining comfort available may be the poet's gift for that kind of "shopping," and for making what she can out of the contents of that disorderly junkshop "where all the ladders start."

That graceful bow to Yeats is not her only acknowledgment of poets who matter to her: there are hints of Emily Dickinson in her sharp observations and crisp imagery, especially in the natural scenes depicted in the book's second division, "Lion's Tooth." There are also insightful references to the lives of women authors, an epigraph from Lorca, and poems addressed to Robert Frost and Deborah Warren.

The double thread that runs through the work of the poets she clearly loves, and through her own, is clear-eyed understanding and acceptance of this world, whatever its shortcomings. Her shapely, gorgeous, musical use of formal patterns—terza rima, the ovillejo, rondeau, pantoum, sonnet and villanelle, to name a few—suggests a loving pursuit of created order, and maybe even a belief—or a desire to believe—in its existence outside of art. In "To the Lightning Bug," the poem from which the book's title is drawn, the poet celebrates that which escapes the common daily destruction that is ordinary life, and finds pleasure in the way we seem to hope for that escape, as if our very hope for it somehow made us, also, provisionally free.

"Her Massive Sandal," whose title is drawn from Millay's sonnet *xlv*, seems to applaud the mathematical approach to reality, the wholly objective basis for aesthetics that led Millay to claim that "Euclid alone has looked on Beauty bare." The sandal belongs to the Muse, who apparently brooks no nonsense. In her own poem, Chandler assures the reader that neither does she:

> I'd rather write that one plus one is two.
> My stance on faith? Euclidean foursquare—
> an abstract God is (n)either here (n)or there,
> and as for love, it can be false or true.

And yet in "Henslow's Sparrow," she softens her stance to this:

> The Henslow's sparrow lives among the sedge
> . . . .
> Or so they say; for I have yet to spy
> the shy, elusive bird, or hear its song
> except in Audubon recordings. I
> admit to shaky faith, but play along.
> And though my yard's a skirl of jays and crows,
> someday it might show up. One never knows.

We're not told whether the speaker's "playing along" is rewarded by the bird's appearance, or by anything at all. Nevertheless, the poet closes her book with a yearning reference to "One who loves," and adds, "I live for nothing less." There is a possibility implied by those words that almost heals the ache they create, and makes the reader wish to be persuaded. But persuaded or not, I love this book, and know that I will return to it again and again—for both the possibility and the ache.

—Rhina P. Espaillat

CONTENTS

II.   *Lion's Tooth*

III.   *Of Change and Time*

IV. *Being a River*

V. *Singularities*

I

Lines of Flight

Oneironaut

It's said that 'lucid dreaming' tames
recurring nightmares. What the bleep—
it's worth a try, like counting sheep.
And as I gave my monsters names,
the unknown landscape backed off, blurred.
I soared across the seven seas,
flew past the rising Pleiades,
pulled into port and slept.   A word,
however, of advice: beware.
Though humdrum dreams may come to lull
the simmering inside your skull,
it's merely a device. The bear,
the bug, bamboozled, may revive.
Sniff out the ruse. Eat you alive.

Lines

For Manon, wherever I may find her

The shop-floor foreman hasn't got a clue
to where the new employee's coming from—
the incense and the ice of Xanadu,
the flame and fury of Byzantium.

He knows for sure she doesn't give a shit
about the piecework in her packing crate—
she checks the clock; at five, she's first to split.
It's no damn wonder that she can't make rate.

He's noticed, too, the woman can be seen
each morning, scribbling in a steno pad,
an island in the boisterous canteen.
Whatever's eating her, she's got it bad.

He's right. Her day job's pretty hard to take
with grace and grit; and she won't last too long,
demanding honey-dew on coffee break;
for no good reason, bursting into song.

66

Along Route 66, connected by
a six-mile stretch of road, two towns align;
one bears his family name, the other mine.
A geographic fluke? Perhaps. But I,
far-flung, uprooted, off the track, embrace
this synchronicity, this table scrap
of happenstance—two dots upon a map
forever linked in existential space.

The decommissioned highway's gone to hell;
and so before it all but disappears,
a faded US atlas, dog-eared to
the State of Oklahoma, guides me through
divergent latitudes and hemispheres
and universes spinning parallel.

Hunger

By January he begins to spot
the whitetail, lying still along the shoulder
of Pennsylvania's roads. As days grow colder,
winter gives the trucker food for thought.
He rolls by, shakes his head as if to say,
Dumb animals, continues on his run
to Scranton, barrels down Route 81,
where loaded semis claim the right-of-way.

He wonders at the annual mistake,
this wandering from woods and hills, and whether,
despairing of alder, tamarack and heather,
a starveling doe, this snowy night, will break
into the clearing, freeze in the headlights' glare,
pay for desire with blood and bones and hair.

Shadow Fish

Great hoarfrost stars
arrive with the shadow fish
clearing the path to dawn.
        —Federico García Lorca, from "Romance sonámbulo"

For the mothers of the disappeared

Here they come, the ravenous sharks of morning,
feasting on the moon and the stars and planets,
swallowing the glimmer of light that's rising
        green in the distance.

Barn owls blink in tacit approval. Cold and
unconcerned, the crickets and frogs keep singing.
Soon the cock will crow, and the fox will charm a
        hare from the woodlot.

Far away the five o'clock whistle blasts its
warning at the desolate crossing. Aspens
shiver. Shadow fish are retreating, silver,
        dragging you with them.

Wing-stroke

For the women in the shelters

His pockets stuffed with Nyjer seed,
he wonders if it's true
that black-capped chickadees will feed
from human hands. They do.

He stands in fascination while
it pecks, relaxed and cool
yet circumspect. He has to smile;
this bird is no one's fool.

It senses something in his touch,
flits from the palm just kissed,
as if it feels the coming clutch
of outstretched hand to fist.

Smart chickadee, to notice in
the blinking of an eye,
the monster in this next of kin
who wouldn't hurt a fly.

Drought

Above our field of stunted corn and thistle,
a lone chimango circles, scouts, homes in
as sure and swift and savage as a missile,
pins down a leveret, rips away its skin,

ignores the terror-stricken eyes, the squeal,
devours the pulsing heart. His thirst now slaked,
he leaves the rest for a carancho's meal.
The land is quivering, crumbling, cracked and caked,

the stream a silent checkerboard of mud,
the well near dry. I pray this lack of water
won't leave me stony at the sight of blood,
of rational, inexorable slaughter.

(Saladillo, Argentina, 2009)

Harrowing

Non est ad astra mollis e terris via.
—Seneca

For Pennsylvania

Her teeming, fertile acres may supply
the world with barley, winter wheat and rye;

but there are other, barren, untilled lands,
for reasons every farmer understands.

It's best to let the bullets, blood and bones
lie undisturbed beneath the soil and stones;

to let the buttercups and meadow-grass
blanket the savagery as seasons pass.

Harvest-time in Shanksville, Nickel Mines
and Gettysburg spills over county lines.

No fences here to keep one out or in;
no gleaners search for hair or teeth or skin.

Yet constellations nightly sow their light
on heaven's fallow fields of anthracite.

Henslow's Sparrow

"Hope" is the thing with feathers
—Emily Dickinson, '#254"

The Henslow's sparrow lives among the sedge
in meadows where the tall grass sighs and bends.
It has been known to skip along the ledge
of surface mines where the escarpment ends.
This delegate of an endangered breed,
whose song is just a whispering refrain,
will perch atop a rosy trumpet weed
unruffled by the darkness and the rain.

Or so they say; for I have yet to spy
the shy, elusive bird, or hear its song,
except in Audubon recordings. I
admit to shaky faith, but play along.
And though my yard's a skirl of jays and crows,
someday it might show up. One never knows.

Ushuaia

In search of the exotic I had flown
as far as Ushuaia. I would see
the penguin and the lenga, for I'd grown
accustomed to the birch, the chickadee.
I crossed the Beagle Channel, met the prince
who sails upon the air, immersed my mind
in images I trusted would convince
myself I'd left the commonplace behind:
the Southern Cross at midnight, and the way
the cordillera bears from west to east,
how wind and weather shift throughout the day—
a poet's fodder, at the very least.

And yet, in retrospect, what I recall
most often when I need the proper noun
is not Olivia or Martial,
but intimations of a downhill town:
a bleak, forsaken prison, silent bogs,
a landscape ravaged by the beaver, frail
impromptu housing, countless scrawny dogs,
a monument to the Malvinas, stale
abandoned factories that bear the brunt
of empty promises, a roadside shrine
to plaster saints, a tourist's waterfront,
complete with tourists from the steamship line.

Though many miles from home, this land would show
that there is really nothing new, indeed,
under the sun, beyond the point of no
return, beyond the *calafate* seed,
beyond all hemispheres, beyond each pole,
beyond the boundaries nations call their own.
The dogs of Ushuaia hound my soul
and gnaw upon it, as they would a bone.

To the Lightning Bug

We'd take your flashing, bitter star,
devise a golden ring;
or trap you in a jelly jar
for the Fairy King.

Plus ça change, the flip cliché;
kids still pinch your light.
Stolen beauty, steal away
in lines of flight!

Delineations

Wild geese flee the coming cold and ice,
  sketching the sky with epic Vs;
    no roundabout for these—
      their route precise.

Starlings in formation never jostle—
  aggregates of living art,
    together yet apart
      in graceful rustle.

Patterns of exuberant design,
  cadenza, cadence, wavelength, arrow,
    slant or straight and narrow—
      theirs, mine.

II

Lion's Tooth

The Deep Season

Good-bye to lavish mercies. Green and lush,
the harmless scam
lies exposed by little deaths—a blush,
a fissured dam,
some mild dismay. Diminishment. The hush
of who I am.

First snow has not yet fallen, and the sun
is stinging bright,
demanding discipline, as one by one,
my once airtight
beloved arguments have come undone,
overnight.

I see the forest. I can see each tree,
the blackened ground,
the field behind, the space inside of me
that makes no sound
yet aches for what I'm not, but need to be—
lost. Then found.

Ballad of the Vernal Equinox

Her cup of coffee's getting cold,
    she's poured herself some gin,
her melancholy uncontrolled,
    her winter-patience thin.

She pulls the curtain back to see
    the bitter silver storm
that's come to numb Sault Ste. Marie
    when weather should be warm.

The snow has stopped, the moon shines hard,
    the wind's a gentle hush.
Coyote drifts into her yard,
    out from the brittle brush.

He stares her down with raw desire,
    his coat a map of scars;
for after all, he's stolen fire
    and spilled a bag of stars.

I know a place where daffodils
    are pushing through the ice,
he hints with all his trickster's skills
    and hopes she won't think twice.

She smiles at him without a flinch,
    reflection in her eyes,
knowing she dare not give an inch
    to one both mad and wise.

A flick of tail—and then he's gone
    without a backward glance,
his one-time offer now withdrawn.
    Too bad. No second chance.

Yet when the geese return and love
    is nowhere to be seen,
she'll scour the woods for traces of
    those brazen spikes of green.

Setback

I'd seen a goldfinch, days were getting mild,
the crocuses were up, and I could hear
the wild geese honking on the pond. Beguiled,
I'd set the garden chairs in place in sheer
delight. The northern winter-spring transition
is never easy, but I'd hoped this year—
Alicia's cancer gone into remission—
that April would be kind. Then we had snow
this afternoon, a boreal admonition:
Not so fast. Not so
fast.
　　　Oh, to be the quiet sort
who bow their heads, accept the status quo,
conceding there's a God and we're his sport,
that winter is so long, and life so short!

Vermont Passage

For Deborah Warren

Wildflowers thrive and form, in mid-July,
a buoyant blue and gold receiving line
the length of Interstate Route 89,
as if to welcome friends and passersby.
But high up in the hillside meadow teems
a purple floret whose divine perfume
makes one forget that roses are in bloom—
mellifluous, the stuff of summer dreams.

And when Vermont's Green Mountains turn to white,
when northern folk see little of the sun,
before the sugar maple sap can run,
when better days attend each bitter night,
I breathe in honeyed memories of clover,
and winter, for a while at least, is over.

For My Granddaughter

Moriah holds my hand in early June.
      Though soon
the lilies we admire will wither, still,
      she will
be happy in our fugitive vignette.
      Forget-
me-nots we'll pick, blue thistle, fern rosette,
hawkweed, trillium, wild columbine:
an afternoon perennially mine,
though soon she will forget.

Dandelion

Love is like the lion's tooth.

—W.B. Yeats, "Words for Music Perhaps—
VII. Crazy Jane Grown Old Looks at the Dancers"

Grown old, she saw a reason to compare
the lowly lion's tooth to love. I'm prone,
as well, to think it highly overblown,
ubiquitous, a gardener's despair.
And though its wine is heady, sweet, beware
of leaves jagged with bitterness. Condone
the mad, outrageous simile, and own
your green intoxications, if you dare.

Don't try to nip it. All you'll ever get
is a wilting weed, dead in half an hour;
but left alone to flourish, rampant, free,
its milky stem will bear the brazen flower
that winks at herbicide and sobriquet,
and dances June away. Defiantly.

Roses and Biscuits

When roses are in bloom
their scent confounds the air.
Her life is a pantoum,
a name, a nom de guerre.

Their scent confounds the air,
it comforts and it wounds;
a name, a nom de guerre,
butterflies, cocoons.

It comforts and it wounds,
the petal and the thorn,
butterflies, cocoons,
the tassels and the corn.

The petal and the thorn,
the curds and whey, the cream;
the tassels and the corn;
the here and now, the dream.

The curds and whey, the cream—
her life is a pantoum—
the here and now, the dream,
when roses are in bloom.

New Hampshire Interval

Upon first visiting The Frost Place, Franconia, New Hampshire

He'd just returned from England, heartened, heady;
he thought he'd make a go of it—he'd farm
and write. This little house was full of charm;
his Morris chair stood by the woodstove, ready.

But woods and mountains intervened; they pined
to cultivate the farmer's friendship, and
he asked them in. For, though he turned the land,
he turned to them when harrowed, undefined,

as often was the case. He did not stay
for very long—the winters were too rough—
and by the second year, he'd had enough:
a summer place it would remain. Today,

I follow others on the footpath where,
nine decades later, one can sense him still,
tapping the frosted trees near Sugar Hill,
speaking to God about the world's despair.

Writ

"Foole," said my Muse to me, "Looke in thy heart and write."
—Sir Philip Sidney, "Astrophel and Stella"

And so I searched, but all that I could see
to write about was this: a vacant room
whose occupants once held a tenancy
of woodstream orchids, where an old perfume
clings to its quiet corners, knows my key
will turn, a frequent caller to a tomb
already ransacked, sifting through debris
only a fool like me would dare exhume.

I've served my warrant, Muse, and I am pleased
to tell you that I've found the smoking gun
you always knew was there. So I have seized
it, tagged and bagged it. Now my work is done.
This evidence I can at last impart—
the delicate forensics of the heart.

Caesura

Between the last triumphant note of fall,
when maples, marigolds and pumpkins vie
for orange jurisdiction, and the rime-
embellished month of Christmas, there he is,

November, stark, severe, demanding all
imagination can afford: a lie
might do the trick; an epic, if there's time.
Anything to fill that void of his.

Cinquefoil

The cinquefoil is the symbol of the beloved daughter, as the leaves bend over to cover the flower when it rains, as a mother would protect her daughter.
      —Cable Natural History Museum, Cable, Wisconsin

For Caitlin

Each spring she'd pick an early pee-the-bed
for me and say,
This for you, for Mother's Day.
I'd put it in a vase, though it was dead,
and praise its droopy yellow head.

Then later, it was *Loves me, loves me not,*
for daisies know
more than a sprig of mistletoe,
or mothers who, it seems, know diddly-squat.
At least that's what I thought she thought.

And when her lilac love had passed away
one winter, she
said it with roses, gracefully;
came home, crossed out her summer wedding day,
chopped off her hair. Faded to grey.

How can a mother's store of moss and cress
soften the hell
of marigold and asphodel?
Can timid snowdrops make a loss hurt less?
Often no. Maybe. Yes.

It's time and thyme we'll need; the flowering reed;
black poplar, white.
Cactus. Yarrow. Love outright.
The weeping willow and the wishing weed.
Those dandelions, gone to seed.

In Nora's Garden

Non semper erit aestas.
　　　　—Erasmus

In Nora's garden, nothing's overgrown;
the phlox and freesias keep their proper place;
no goldenrod, no florid overblown
rugosas spoil the cultivated grace.
In Nora's garden, hummingbirds and bees
find ample sustenance all summer long;
her suet feeders swing from maple trees
whose visitors repay her gift in song.
It wasn't always so. I can remember
when dandelions ruled. My mirthful neighbor
could not have cared less, April through September,
about the weather or the fruits of labor.
In Nora's garden, everything is plum;
her hedge against whatever else may come.

III

Of Change and Time

The Loiterers

Each morning at exactly nine o'clock,
our fellowship of grizzle-headed men
meets at McDonald's, métro Frontenac.

We take our customary seats, and then,
despite the posted warning, *PAS DE FLÂNAGE*,
drink discount coffee for an hour or two.

Surrounded by a motley entourage
of East-End Montrealers, we outdo
each other with our lively poppycock.

Long since returned from distant Neverlands,
we turn a deaf ear to the ticking clock.
The manager is kind. He understands

our *joie de vivre*, our order of the day;
refills our cups, and grants that it's no crime
to hold our own, and though we overstay,

to squander what we've left of change and time.

Fatuity

She stood behind me in the check-out queue
last Saturday. She mentally weighed in
on items in my shopping cart. I knew
her thoughts: *It's no small wonder she's not thin
like me. Look at that junk food - cookies, chips,
that pint of Häagen-Dazs, those salted nuts . . .*
She sized me up and down from head to hips
and measured both our budgets and our butts.

Clairvoyant she was not. Had she but seen
as with the scanner's unassuming eye,
she might have figured out a lifetime lean
and hard. Before I wheeled my week's supply
of relish out into the parking lot,
I whispered, *Lady, this is all I've got.*

Quittance

Somewhat after Colossians 2:13-14

I had a fortune, but it's spent;
I haven't saved a single cent.
I've pawned my soul to pay the rent.

No stocks, no bonds, no pension plan;
my nest egg's in the frying pan.
Hey, can I have that soda can?

I should have rationed, squared my debts;
I should have written off regrets.
I should have rolled my cigarettes.

Instead, I let the well run dry,
lived high-off-the-hog (and I mean high).
I'm down-and-out. Oh, by the by,

since all my bills are overdue
and I've no source of revenue,
God, will you scrap my IOU?

Boots

The grown-ups called her Boots. Stilettoed. Brash.
Hayna Valley girl. All skin-on-bone.
Afternoons, impassive as a stone,
she'd strut downtown to trade her time for cash
(they said) from college boys. As rumors flew, it
made me perk my ears. Living next door,
I learned new words like *incest, jailbait, whore.*
As for her real name, I never knew it.

And then she moved. The Amy Vanderbilts
sang hallelujahs. Thanked their lucky stars.
Boots could not belong. She came from Mars,
thumbing her nose at coffee klatches, quilts,
silk stockings, and the picket-fences of
Earth's fond contrivances passed off as love.

sub rosa

There were two: shy "Emilie", quiet "Ellis".
One assumed a masculine name to mask it;
one dropped sweets and messages in a basket
               over the trellis.

Boy or bee, the Belle would take rules and bend them
with her slant on rhythm and rhyme and nectar.
As for Ellis, no one would dare respect her
               should she offend them

with a tale of blustering heights of passion
written by a maidenly preacher's daughter.
One despaired of finding an imprimatur,
               wearing an ashen

wardrobe, watching, stitching her words together.
Dreams of Gondal! Dreams of a secret lover!
Still the skittish poet(ess) runs for cover:
               birds of a feather

may in mortal fear of the prejudicial,
even now, when tempted to seek admission,
approbation, countenance, recognition,
               use the initial.

Assembly

Martha lugs a battered cardboard box
of photographs down from the attic shelf.
She sorts them into categories—blocks
of time momentous only to herself.
They seem to settle into classic themes:
vacations, birthdays, friends, 4th of Julys,
graduations, weddings, softball teams,
reunions, Christmases. Hellos. Good-byes.

For forty years now, Martha's been a wife
and mother. Still, these Kodak legacies
in some way bear false witness to her life.
She puts the box away. The other she's
still unaccounted for in every scene—
each afterward, before and in-between.

The Gambler

He drops another token in
and hopes he hears the jackpot bell.
He's sure this time. He's got to win.
He drops another token in,
then watches as the rollers spin
and stop. So close! Oh, what the hell—
he drops another token in
and hopes . . . he hears the jackpot bell!

Where All the Ladders Start

I visited her shop this afternoon
to rummage through the clutter and the schlock.
As usual, old tins and jars were strewn
pell-mell across the floor. *I'm out of stock
in dancing bears,* she yammered, *but I've got
a thousand smithereens up on the shelf.
I'll take a shiny penny for the lot.*

I knew I'd have to fetch them for myself;
and yet, the price was right. I filled my bags
with broken glass, with beads and brittle bones;
then for good measure, reams of tattered rags,
a rusty can, a box of sticks and stones:
the rudiments of memory and art—
the poems howling from my shopping cart.

I Had Some Things

A cento from Emily Dickinson

I had some things that I called mine—
I asked no other thing—
I lost a world the other day—
I years had been from home—

I thought that nature was enough—
I took one draught of life—
I watched the moon around the house—
I could not drink it, sweet—

I felt my life with both my hands—
I gave myself to him—
I could suffice for him, I knew—
I think I was enchanted—

I was a phoebe, nothing more—
I stepped from plank to plank—
I learned at least what home could be—
I am alive, I guess—

Irène: A Portrait

Mademoiselle Irène Cahen D'Anvers,
        by Pierre-Auguste Renoir, 1880

She looks complaisant, with her dainty hands
demurely on her lap. Red hair cascades
below her waist. Her countenance demands
one disregard the backdrop's somber shades

to focus on the eyes, the vacant gaze,
the incandescent skin, the perfect nose,
the brow she has a tendency to raise,
perhaps in mild impatience with the pose.

And then, there is the mouth—the winsome curve,
a smile almost incongruously sly.
But now let's take a closer look. Observe:
Irène will bear two offspring who will die,

one in the downing of his fighter plane,
one in the holocaust at Auschwitz.
Not yet sophisticated, cool, urbane,
in blissful ignorance the young girl sits.

Renoir declared that art must aim to trace
the pleasant, pretty side of life; and with
a stroke of genius, turned a commonplace
into an icon in the realm of myth.

Mother's Day

On Sunday evening after the party ends
and family have gone, you ache to say
how you can't bear this gathering each May.
Your thoughtful husband usually sends
a rose bouquet, but changed his mind this year:
a special gift, it makes your finger shine
with emerald and ruby. *Too much wine,*
he banters as he wipes away your tear.

But you and I know, Mother, what he can't—
your April foolishness; how bit by bit
they snipped me out of you, "took care of it";
how through the years I've been your confidante,
the reason for this night's unraveling—
the garnet missing from the mother's ring.

To the Man on Mansfield Street

I have imagined countless reasons for
your sleeping on the hotel heating vent—
a lengthy layoff, months of unpaid rent,
a gambling debt, divorce, a private war . . .

Or was it something darker, maybe drink,
a need to fill your veins with heroin;
insanity, a secret or a sin
you wouldn't whisper to a priest or shrink?

The morning traffic soon will wake you up;
you'll check there's nothing missing from your bag;
you'll bind your blisters with a dirty rag
and later gauge the clinking in your cup.

I see the bright-eyed boy you surely were;
I see the tender infant, newly-born,
the Baby who, before the cross and thorn,
was given gold and frankincense and myrrh.

Unlike the offerings of wiser men,
all that I give you is a cigarette,
the time of day, some change, my mute regret
that begs to differ with the word, *Amen.*

IV

Being a River

Susquehanna

For Wilkes-Barre

The Susquehanna runs its ancient course,
passing by and passing up my town.
Being a river, it carries no remorse
for flood, for mud, or for the tumble-down.
Being a river, it has a total lack
of reverence for triangles of stars,
or for those aged breaker boys with black-
choked lungs drowning their pain in local bars.
And in its rush to reach the Chesapeake,
it sweeps to Maryland; it swirls, it pulls,
not knowing it was once an upstate creek.
The Susquehanna has no truck with fools
like me who spurn its blighted, brown advice,
wavering near its waters. Thinking twice.

Of Things Past

Briefly thyself remember...
    —William Shakespeare, *King Lear,* Act 4, Scene 6

I. 99 Bottles of Beer on the Wall

That summer when I couldn't see
for grief—for who could guarantee
he'd ever walk again?—I'd sing
this song and pump my rusty swing,
till every bottle left the wall,
then start *da capo* (it was all
or nothing) in a voice, though small,
as if the magic chant might bring
my father walking back to me.

II. Madeleine Moment

Ah, there's Poughkeepsie. Nineteen fifty-four.
I skip along the Hudson. As the boats
go by, my father calls to me and quotes,
'Still waters run deep', as clearly as before
his polio; when, like this chewing-gum,
my life was one sweet, succulent cliché;
where, dauntless in the sun that could not stay,
he climbed the evergreen, I ate the plum.

Joy Ride

I cheated death—oh, what a thrill!—
that summer afternoon I sped
my brand-new Schwinn down Beaumont hill
right through the stop sign, and instead

of braking, met a fateless day.
Why did I do it? I was one
who brushed her teeth, put toys away,
but thought some freedom might be fun.

And so it was, till guilt set in:
grim thoughts—a crowd, a mangled waif,
my disobedience, a sin
I never did confess.   It's safe

to be an easy rider; blah
to take the road most traveled by.
For years now I've obeyed the law.
But once I was a butterfly.

Docga

My dog has heard what others never hear:
ravings at the ceiling in the dark;
she smells the fear
I sweat in that same dream
of lupine shadows worse than bite or bark.
She paws at me and whimpers when I scream.

My dog has tasted salt upon my hands;
she's licked it from the wrinkles on my face.
She understands
the frantic, buried bone,
the need to find the perfect hiding place,
the need to have a refuge of one's own.

My dog has viewed me naked, not a stitch
to mask the striae. She could not care less;
she's an old bitch
like me. But not a day
(or week) goes by that she can't see I dress
without success, and loves me anyway.

My dog keeps life's inhuman hounds at bay.

Gia Dinh

For Thomas F. Smith, Jr., 1945 - 1968

In Washington there's bugger-all
to lure me down from Montreal.
And yet, when it was done I came
to tell and touch and trace your name,
to taste the wormwood and the gall.

The Tet Offensive saw you fall
near Hoc Mon Bridge. Still, maggots crawl
and feast and life is much the same
in Washington.

It's strange the things I best recall—
you hated Ringo, I loved Paul.
You dreamed you'd pitch the perfect game
like Koufax. What a bloody shame.
I weep beside this granite wall
in Washington.

Marah's Waters

He lifts me from the wheelchair to the water,
my arms entwined around his neck. A wave
breaks on us, aged father, aging daughter.
He is too *caballero*, much too brave
to show the strain, the effort it must take;
but the charade is obvious to me.
Like every summer, then, I smile and fake
indifference to the fast-encroaching sea.

We're laughing, floating, buoyant in the swell
of Río de la Plata's tidal flow;
like other tossed things—seaweed, sand and shell—
we hold our own against the undertow.
And when at last the shore recedes from view,
the ballast of our hearts will bear us true.

(Piriápolis, Uruguay, 2004)

Gathering

My house was full an hour ago,
a symphony of harmony and laughter.
I shiver at the sound of what's come after—
music, calando, low
echoes off the walls, a slow
rumor in the wind of real weather
warning me that I must hold together,
as I arpeggio.

Elderberry Tale

Once upon a time at summer's end,
without specific plans to fill my day,
I sauntered to her house. I would pretend
I'd never heard the stories of the way

the week divided into different chores.
Her gravel voice and knotted hands explained
the wringing of the wash, the hard-scrubbed floors,
the kneading and the knitting. As she strained

the mash of berries, crimson droplets bled
in trickles to a saucepan on the stove.
The secret's in the knowing how, she said,
to measure sugar, cinnamon and clove.

For happily-ever-afters, her advice
has come in handy. As I stir my brew—
the cauldron simmering with sweet and spice—
I add a pinch of snail, a frog or two.

Bottom of the Ninth

Mid-afternoon, church over, Dad and I
settled in the living room to read
the Sunday paper with its stout supply
of inserts. He supposed (and I agreed)
there'd be no war—advisors would advise;
Nixon would trounce Kennedy; of course
Luthuli'd never win the Nobel Prize.

With Mazeroski's brilliant tour de force
undreamed of, weeks away, Dad coolly aced
the crossword, as I scanned the comic strips,
the fashion pages and the book reviews.
In time this confidence would prove misplaced,
as often happens with apprenticeships.
We were so sure our Yankees couldn't lose.

(September 1960)

When in Lourdes

I lingered on the little bridge across
the Gave de Pau, whose waters, in the sweep
of April, coursed beneath it. At a loss
for words, I scrutinized the crowd, the cheap
boutiques, the bottles for domestic use,
but still sought out the consecrated sites.
My fragile faith becoming less diffuse,
I prayed beside the grotto, walked the night's
procession, visited the cold Cachot,
lit a candle, bought some rosary beads,
beamed beatific for a day or so,
then left for Paris on the train that speeds
its passengers back to reality,
my pilgrimage diminished by regrets—
the miracles that were not meant to be,
the plastic, Made-in-China Bernadettes.

Matryoshka

What made me buy the nested Russian doll
whose faded paint and fractured wooden frame
had doomed her to a yard sale? Had her fall
from grace inspired a longing to reclaim
for her, for fifty cents, some lost esteem?
Or would the curious plaything prove to be
a conversation piece? No, it would seem
I brought the pregnant outcast home for me.

For women I had tried so long to trace,
Matryoshka was a tangible motif;
same yet separate, I knew the face,
gave up each grievance, sanctioned every grief.
Restored, they stand here, echoing one another—
mother, daughter, mother, daughter, mother.

Journey

We love the things we love for what they are.
—Robert Frost, "Hyla Brook"

From Pennsylvania she has traveled far,
yet home is in the valley and the hills.
She loves the things she loves for what they are.

The watchful moon once tracked a Pullman car
past dingy culm banks and the linen mills
of Pennsylvania. She has traveled far

into the sunset, toward the evening star,
spent lavish pesos, pink two-dollar bills,
and loved. Some things she loves for where they are,

yearning, like dyads on a steel guitar,
for rivers, be they Canada's, Brazil's
or Pennsylvania's. Though she's traveled far,

she's always thought in terms of *au revoir*,
a promise that (if dreams count) she fulfills.
Those souls she loved and loves know who they are,

and leaving them behind has left a scar,
a tolerance for pain and sleeping pills.
From Pennsylvania she has traveled far
and wide. She weeps, but loves things as they are.

V

Singularities

Missing

For Cédrika

It started out like any other day.
You got up early, telephoned your friends,
had breakfast, waved good-bye, then sped away
to Parc Chapais. And there your story ends.

They found your bike. Some girls described a man
who claimed he'd lost his dog the day before.
You would have felt his loss, though others ran.
It's been so long. They don't search anymore.

A wild imagination's unforgiving . . .
sometimes I almost hope that you are dead.
Yet there's the slimmest chance you're somewhere. Living.
The case is cold, not closed. And so, instead
of granting sad conclusions long foregone,
I leave the door unlocked, the porch light on.

Supernova

A burnished afternoon. Why dull it with
a lapse to metaphor
or scientific fact, or myth,
or say there's more

to life than what the naked eye perceives
or what the ear can hear?
Why paraphrase the shushing leaves,
the swoosh of deer?

Why try to parse the chirrup of the birds
or posit love's a stew
of enzymes? Why resort to words
when hush will do?

As afternoon declines to dusk I stand
uncertain and perplexed,
your ashes in my trembling hand.
I ask, *What next?*

Then grant the constancy of truths and laws,
of motive, meaning, mind;
of logic, reason, purpose, cause;
because I find

it's easier to release you, as I must,
less harrowing by far,
knowing that all human dust
was once a star.

Flammarion Woodcut Pilgrim Redux

He scans the sky and wonders if the Hubble
will burst (or not) the quintessential bubble,
plotting new data on a deep field chart
light years removed from any human heart.

Her Massive Sandal

You have no idea how much poetry there is in the calculation of a table of logarithms!
—Jane Muir, *Of Men and Numbers*

Don't ask me to describe the color blue
or to portray the flavor of a pear;
to explicate the texture of the air
or draw a contour map of Timbuktu.
I'd rather write that one plus one is two.
My stance on faith? Euclidean foursquare—
an abstract God is (n)either here (n)or there,
and as for love, it can be false or true.

In cold and calculating, clear, exact
equations, I approach infinity
while you are left to reason with your heart.
And yet in symbols signifying fact
we share a common tongue, a symmetry,
the pure delineations of our art.

Prayer on the Pampas

Los Pueblitos. A million miles from Buenos Aires. Slivers of gold shimmer through the tall wooden shutters onto the bed sheet.

we are the dust motes
riding on the morning light—
wayward iotas

A stone fish arcs at each cardinal point on the hundred-year-old fountain. The sundial's shadow is past noon. Torpor.

cool water plashes
we sit and sip tereré—
a stonefly flits by

Behind the soya fields and cow pastures, the evening sky bleeds orange into purple. Jasmine and eucalyptus fuse.

looking to the west
she whispers a secret wish—
a green granada

Ñacurutú begins his elegy. Wind chimes plink. The swirl of the Earth palpable. Stars spill, Polaris swallowed by latitudes.

she guides me to Crux—
we'll pilgrimage to Luján
when the sun rises

68

Endgame

While trailing clouds it never crossed my mind—
that final, gruesome fact. Of course I knew
that old folks passed away. Sometimes behind
great-uncles we would ride, a retinue
of cousins pressed into the somber suit,
of grown-ups whispering a word, *bequest*.
And then the war. Our Tommy's last salute.
The real thing. No, this was not a test.

No airy intimations. Death had found
a grudging playmate for his hide-and-seek.
With butterflies I skirt the hallowed ground,
safe for another day, another week.
How will it end, and where?—my tainted thought.
When will I hear him cry, *"READY OR NOT!"*?

∞

He shakes his head, tsk-tsks at the trompe l'oeil,
unfazed by magic;
wrings his hands and utters *Oy yoy yoy!*
at fuzzy logic.

But when infinity falls in the mix
he'll never risk it;
he holds his nose and raids his bag of tricks
for the lemniscate.

Ruins

I pause to rest beside the temple of
Antonius and Faustina. All this stone
and sunlight, mingled with the leaden drone
of tour guides, the oppressive push-and-shove
of camera-wielding pilgrims, makes me search
for sanctuary; and an olive tree—
September 12, 2001 A.D.—
provides the hushed asylum of a church.

This peaceful corner that the tour left out
might tempt another traveler, by and by,
to view the Forum with a quiet eye
and think it something to write home about.
As I am doing now; except I scrawl
Wish I were there on postcards that portray
an artist's sketch of Rome before the fall,
its columns shining in the brilliant day.

Eleven

players on a soccer team
stars in Joseph's second dream

odd reversible and prime
dimensions (counting space and time)

pipers piping, salt (Na)
month day hour Veteran's Day

goat's hair curtains ripped apart
ounce-weight of the human heart

twelve less Judas, David's men
pearls and tears from Swinburne's pen

heartbreak (on a scale of ten)

Spirit

How desolate, exposed, the living room,
our customary spruce out by the curb.
How green of me to think, expect, presume
that I'd feel festive as a Hallmark blurb
this time. No elders at the fireside,
I sigh, no kneeling oxen. It is clear
I've failed again, although I really tried
to trim my tree sufficiently this year.

In January's pallid, lifeless light,
with April pending like a clockwork star,
the Magi gone, the family in flight,
I value sugar-plums for what they are.
Yet I shall pack each ornament with care
and stock up on some half-priced angel hair.

Lost and Found

A key, a button, a leather glove.
First love.

A friend to cancer, a voice to grief.
An old belief.

An arrowhead, a perfect shell.
The first bluebell.

The river's source, a taste for ink.
Hope, I think.

Singularities

*For what man knoweth the things of a man, save the
spirit of man which is in him? Even so the things of God
knoweth no man, but the Spirit of God.*
    —1 Corinthians 2:11

The universe is old. As for its birth—
when space-time burst in from infinity,
before the Pleiades and planet Earth,
before the tale of serpent, man and tree—
an unsolved mystery. The easy stuff
came later. Astrophysicists still try
to explicate the stars. It's not enough.
We want to know not only what, but why.

And then there is The End, when all dimensions
may drop away into a hole as dark
as nought; when truth will nullify inventions,
consuming every quark and antiquark;
when present, past and future coalesce
in One who loves. I live for nothing less.

Notes

"Oneironaut": the root, *oneiro*, comes from the Greek word for "dream".

"Docga" is the Old English origin of the word "dog". Roughly translated, it means "powerful breed of dog."

"Drought": the *chimango* is a common raptor in southern South America; the *carancho* is a carrion-eating bird, also native to that region.

"Harrowing": *Non est ad astra mollis e terris via.* Latin for *"There is no smooth way from the earth to the stars."* (Seneca)

"Ushuaia": the lenga is a deciduous tree native to the southern Andes range; Olivia is a mountain peak and Martial is a glacier, both tourist attractions in Ushuaia.

"In Nora's Garden": *Non semper erit aestas.* Latin for *"It will not always be summer."* (Erasmus)

"The Loiterers": *PAS DE FLÁNAGE* - French for: *NO LOITERING.*

"Marah's Waters": *caballero*—Spanish for *gentleman(ly)*.

"Mother's Day": the garnet is the traditional birthstone for the month of January.

"Missing" is dedicated to Cédrika Provencher, a girl from Trois-Rivières, Québec, who has been missing since July 31, 2007.

"Prayer on the Pampas": tereré is the iced version of *yerba mate*, a bitter herbal drink shared among friends in South America; Ñacurutú is the indigenous name given to the Great Horned Owl in Argentina; Crux is the Southern Cross; the cathedral at Luján is a place of pilgrimage near Buenos Aires.

"∞": the lemniscate, ∞, is the symbol for infinity. From Latin lēmniscus, *ribbon*, from Greek lēmniskos, perhaps from Lēmnos.

Author Photo by Linda May

Catherine Chandler, an American poet born in New York City and raised in Pennsylvania, completed her graduate studies at McGill University in Montreal, where she has lectured in the Department of Languages and Translation for many years. She is the winner of the Howard Nemerov Sonnet Award.

Her poems, interviews, essays and English translations from French and Spanish have been published in numerous print and online journals and anthologies in the United States, the United Kingdom, Canada and Australia. She is coeditor of *Passages* (The Greenwood Centre for Living History), and author of two chapbooks, *For No Good Reason* and *All or Nothing*.